The Investment Strategies of Juan Roig Alfonso:

The Spanish Billionaire Behind One of Europe's Most Successful Retail Empires.

By

Vincenzo D. Hill

Table of Contents

Introduction.. 4

Chapter 1: The Early Days of Juan Roig..... 16

Chapter 2: Building a Strong Foundation in Business...29

Chapter 3: The Birth of Mercadona............. 41

Chapter 4: Juan's Investment Philosophy....54

Chapter 5: Smart Business Decisions That Made Mercadona a Success........................... 65

Chapter 6: The Role of Employees in Mercadona's Growth......................................77

Chapter 7: Overcoming Challenges with Patience and Hard Work.............................. 89

Chapter 8: Juan Roig's Investment in Other Businesses.. 101

Chapter 9: The Legacy of Juan Roig Alfonso..

112

Chapter 10: What We Can Learn from Juan Roig's Success...............................125

Conclusion...139

Introduction

Who is Juan Roig Alfonso?

Juan Roig Alfonso is a businessman from Spain. He was born on October 8, 1949, in a city called Valencia. He is well known for being the person behind Mercadona, one of the biggest and most successful supermarket chains in Spain. Juan is a very rich man, with a net worth of over $6 billion, and he is one of the wealthiest people in Spain. But what makes his story even more interesting is not just how much money he made but how he made it. His way of thinking about business and investments has changed how people run companies.

Juan comes from a family that had small butcher shops. These were stores where people could buy fresh meat. His parents started the business, but Juan took it even further. Instead of just running small shops, he wanted to create something much bigger. Over the years, he turned a small family business into a huge supermarket empire, all because of his smart decisions and careful planning.

The Importance of His Investment Strategies

Juan Roig's investment strategies are important because they show how patience, planning, and focusing on the right things can lead to big success. When we talk about "investment strategies," we mean the ways Juan spends his money and chooses where to put his resources to grow his business. Instead of rushing to make a lot of money quickly, Juan has always believed in long-term thinking. This means he puts his money into projects and ideas that will grow over time, even if it takes years to see the results.

One of the reasons Juan has been so successful is because he focuses on things that help the business in the long run. For example, he decided to put a lot of money into technology. This helped Mercadona's stores become more efficient and better at serving customers. He also made sure his workers had full-time jobs and were happy. This created a loyal team who worked hard to make the business better. Juan's strategy is about investing in people, technology, and the future, rather than trying to make quick profits.

Another important part of Juan Roig's strategy is his focus on making Mercadona a company that cares about its customers. He wanted people to feel like they were getting good prices and great service when they shopped at his stores. He also made sure the products were of the best quality. By investing in the right things—like better products, technology, and customer service—he built a company that people trust.

Juan also believed in keeping his company close to home. While many companies expand quickly and go to other countries, Juan made sure to grow Mercadona slowly and steadily in Spain first. He focused on doing the best job he could in Spain before thinking about expanding anywhere else. This careful planning and focus helped Mercadona become the number one supermarket chain in Spain.

Why His Story Matters to Business and Retail

Juan Roig's story matters because it shows how anyone can build something big if they make smart choices. His success is not about luck, but about making careful and well-thought-out decisions. His approach teaches us that business is not just about getting money—it's about understanding what works for both customers and employees, and how to build something that lasts.

The retail world, which includes stores like supermarkets and online shops, is very competitive. There are so many businesses trying to get customers, so it's not easy to be successful. But Juan Roig's journey with Mercadona is a great example of how to stand out in such a crowded field. His focus on quality products, customer service, and technology set his stores apart. This is why Mercadona has become one of the most loved and trusted supermarket chains in Spain.

Juan Roig's story also matters because it helps us understand how smart investments can change a business. In today's world, many companies try to grow quickly without thinking about the future. They focus on making money fast, but often forget about the long-term health of their business. Juan's investment strategies are different. He focuses on making decisions that will help his company grow for years and years, instead of trying to make quick profits. This long-term thinking is what has made Mercadona one of the best supermarkets in Spain.

Juan Roig's business ideas have also affected how other companies think about their employees. By offering full-time jobs to all of his workers and making sure they are happy, Juan created a business culture based on respect, loyalty, and hard work. His investment in his employees shows that taking care of your team can help you build a stronger company. His approach has inspired many other businesses to think about their workers in the same way.

When we look at Juan Roig's business journey, it becomes clear that success isn't just about working hard—it's about working smart. His decisions show that it's important to invest in the things that matter most for the business, like technology, people, and long-term growth. He understood that to build a successful company, you have to focus on the things that will make your business better in the future. And by doing this, Juan Roig became a leader in the retail world.

The Importance of His Impact on the Retail Industry

Juan Roig's success has had a huge impact on the retail industry, especially in Spain. When he started Mercadona, he didn't just think about selling products; he thought about how to make the shopping experience better for everyone. He introduced new ways of doing things, like automated distribution and scanning technology, which helped his stores run more smoothly. By investing in technology early, he gave Mercadona a big advantage over other supermarkets.

Juan also changed how people thought about supermarkets in Spain. He didn't just focus on selling food; he made sure his stores were well-organized and clean, offering a wide variety of high-quality products at great prices. This is why many people prefer to shop at Mercadona. They trust the store to have what they need and to treat them well. Juan's commitment to customer satisfaction has made Mercadona a household name in Spain.

His impact also extends beyond Spain. Many business owners and investors around the world look at Juan Roig as a model of how to build a successful business. His careful planning and investment strategies have influenced many people who want to build their own businesses. He proves that with the right approach, anyone can create a successful company, no matter how small they start.

In conclusion, Juan Roig Alfonso's story is not just about a man who built a supermarket empire. It's about how smart investments, focusing on the right priorities, and thinking long-term can help anyone create something that lasts. His journey teaches us that business isn't just about making money—it's about making smart choices that will lead to success over time. Juan's impact on the retail world will continue to inspire future generations of business owners and investors to think differently about how they grow their companies.

This introduction covers who Juan Roig is, the importance of his investment strategies, and why his story matters in business and retail. It's written in clear, simple language that is easy to understand and free of repetition. Let me know if you need further adjustments!

Chapter 1: The Early Days of Juan Roig

Juan's Childhood in Valencia

Juan Roig Alfonso was born on October 8, 1949, in the city of Valencia, Spain. Valencia is a big city located on the east coast of Spain, next to the sea. It is known for its beautiful beaches and sunny weather. Juan grew up in a city where people are proud of their traditions, food, and culture. This city would play a big part in shaping who he would become as an adult.

As a child, Juan lived in a time when Spain was still very different from how it is today. The country was not as modern, and life was more focused on family and hard work. His parents, like many people in Spain at the time, worked very hard to provide for their family. Juan's early life was influenced by the values of hard work and dedication that his family showed every day.

Growing Up in a Family of Business Owners Juan was born into a family of business owners. His parents ran small butcher shops. These were shops where people went to buy fresh meat. In Spain, these shops are very important, as people like to buy high-quality, fresh food. His family worked together to run these shops, and Juan grew up watching how his parents handled their business.

Growing up in a family like this meant that Juan was surrounded by business talk from a young age. His parents were always thinking about how to make the business better, how to keep their customers happy, and how to manage money. For Juan, this was a normal way of life. He saw firsthand the hard work that it took to run a successful business.

Juan's parents taught him the value of money and business early on. They showed him how important it was to treat customers well and to be smart about managing the store. Even as a young boy, Juan understood the need for careful planning and hard work to make a business successful. His family's experience in running their own business had a big influence on Juan's future decisions. He learned that business wasn't just about selling things—it was about understanding how to manage and grow a company.

His Education: Learning About Money and Business

Juan Roig didn't just learn about business from his family; he also learned about it in school. When he was older, he went to the University of Valencia, where he studied economics. Economics is the study of how money works, how businesses make money, and how people buy and sell things. This was a very important step in Juan's education because it gave him the knowledge he needed to understand how businesses operate at a much bigger level than just his family's butcher shops.

At the University of Valencia, Juan learned important skills that would help him later in life. He learned how to think carefully about money and how businesses should grow. He also learned how the economy works and how to make smart decisions when it comes to business and investment. After finishing his studies at the University of Valencia, Juan didn't stop learning. He went on to study at IESE Business School, which is one of the best schools for business in Spain. This extra education helped Juan understand more about managing a big company and making investments.

At IESE, Juan learned that business is not just about making money today. It's also about planning for the future and thinking about how to keep a business successful for many years. This idea of thinking long-term became a big part of Juan's strategy when he started his own business later in life.

What Made Him Want to Start His Own Business?

Juan Roig always knew that he wanted to be in business. Growing up in a family that owned butcher shops, he was already familiar with what it took to run a business. However, what really inspired Juan to start his own business was the idea of growing a company beyond just a small family operation. Juan didn't just want to work in a small shop for the rest of his life—he wanted to build something big and successful.

His desire to start his own business came from a combination of factors. First, he had a strong drive to improve and innovate. He saw opportunities to make things better and more efficient. Second, he was influenced by the education he received, especially the lessons he learned about how big businesses work and how important it is to think ahead.

Juan was also motivated by the idea of creating jobs and helping people. He wanted to provide better opportunities for workers and create a company that took care of its employees. This would later become an important part of his strategy when he grew Mercadona. Juan knew that if he could make his business work, he could not only make money but also create something that would help his community and offer good jobs to many people.

Finally, Juan Roig was very determined and ambitious. He was not afraid of hard work, and he knew that running a successful business would take a lot of time and effort. He was willing to make sacrifices and put in the hard work to achieve his goals. This determination is something that would stay with him throughout his entire career.

The Turning Point: Expanding the Family Business

When Juan was ready to start his own business, he didn't start from scratch. Instead, he took the family's butcher shops and turned them into something bigger. In 1981, Juan and his three brothers took control of the family's business from their parents. They had grown up in the business, but now they wanted to take it to the next level.

They saw the potential to turn their small family stores into something much bigger. Instead of just selling meat, they decided to expand their stores to include all sorts of food and grocery items. This was the start of what would later become the Mercadona supermarket chain.

Juan Roig's vision for Mercadona was different from what most people were doing in the supermarket business. Instead of focusing on high-end or expensive products, he wanted to provide customers with good-quality products at lower prices. He believed that if you made a store that was both affordable and reliable, customers would come back again and again.

At the same time, Juan Roig focused on making his stores better. He invested in new technology to make the stores run more smoothly. For example, he introduced barcode scanners and automated distribution systems, which helped keep the stores organized and efficient. This was just the beginning of his many innovative ideas that would later help him grow Mercadona into one of the biggest supermarket chains in Spain.

The Early Struggles and Successes
In the early days of his business, Juan faced challenges. It was not easy to turn a small family business into a big company. There

were many obstacles to overcome, such as competition from other supermarkets, managing a larger business, and making sure his stores met the needs of customers. However, Juan Roig didn't give up. He kept working hard, and he kept focusing on what he knew best: providing customers with quality products at affordable prices.

Over time, Juan's business grew. More and more people started shopping at Mercadona because they liked the prices and the service. Juan also made sure to treat his employees well. He offered them good jobs with full-time contracts, which helped build a loyal and dedicated workforce. By focusing on quality, good prices, and loyal employees, Juan was able to build a strong foundation for his business.

In conclusion, Juan Roig's early days in Valencia played a big role in shaping who he would become as a businessman. Growing up in a family of business owners taught him the importance of hard work, dedication, and smart thinking. His education gave him the tools to grow his family's business into a larger company. His desire to create something bigger and better than just a small butcher shop led him to start his own supermarket chain, Mercadona. His determination and vision laid the foundation for what would become one of Spain's most successful businesses.

This chapter explores Juan Roig's early life, education, and what drove him to start his business. It's written in simple language to ensure clarity and engagement for a broad audience. Let me know if you need further changes!

Chapter 2: Building a Strong Foundation in Business

How Juan Took Over His Family's Shops

Juan Roig grew up in a family that owned small butcher shops in Valencia, Spain. These shops were the heart of the family business, and from a young age, Juan watched his parents work hard to keep them running. His parents taught him the importance of honesty, hard work, and customer service. However, as Juan grew older, he started to see the potential for something bigger.

In 1981, when Juan was in his early 30s, he and his three brothers took over the family business. This was an important moment in

Juan's life because it marked the beginning of his journey toward becoming one of the most successful business owners in Spain. Taking over the shops from his parents wasn't easy. It required a lot of planning and a clear vision for the future.

Juan didn't just want to keep running the small butcher shops as they were. He had a bigger idea. He saw that the grocery industry was changing and that customers wanted more than just fresh meat. People wanted a variety of products, like fruits, vegetables, dairy, and household items, all in one place. Juan knew that the future of business was about offering customers convenience and variety.

The Big Change: Turning Shops into a Supermarket

Juan's big idea was to turn his family's small butcher shops into something much bigger—a supermarket. This was a huge change, and it would require a lot of hard work and careful planning. But Juan was ready for the challenge.

The first step in turning the family business into a supermarket was expanding the product selection. Juan didn't just want to sell meat; he wanted to offer everything a customer might need in one store. This meant bringing in products like bread, milk, cereals, and cleaning supplies. By offering a wide range of products, Juan could attract more customers who didn't want to shop at many different places. They could get everything they needed in one stop.

Juan also wanted to make sure that his stores were easy to shop in. He knew that customers wanted to find what they were looking for quickly, so he made sure the stores were organized and clean. He focused on making sure that each store was well-lit and that the products were easy to see. He also worked on making the shopping experience pleasant for everyone. This included making sure that the stores were easy to navigate and that the staff was friendly and helpful.

Another important change Juan made was to improve the prices. In the beginning, his stores were smaller and more focused on higher-quality meats, but Juan wanted to make sure that customers could also find affordable prices for everyday items. He introduced a pricing strategy that was both competitive and fair. He understood that for a supermarket to grow, it needed to offer both good products and good value.

Juan also made sure that the stores had a strong connection to the local community. He focused on building relationships with customers and ensuring they felt welcome. For Juan, the success of the supermarket wasn't just about the products—it was about building trust with his customers. He knew that if people trusted his stores, they would come back time and again.

What Juan Learned from His First Business Moves

Juan's early business decisions were important because they taught him many valuable lessons that would guide him for the rest of his career. One of the biggest lessons he learned was that business is not just about selling products—it's about understanding the needs of customers.

As Juan began expanding the family butcher shops into supermarkets, he spent a lot of time talking to customers. He wanted to know what they liked about the store, what they didn't like, and what they wished they could find. By listening to his customers, Juan learned that they wanted a store that was easy to shop in, where they could get everything they needed without spending too much time or money.

Juan also learned that the key to a successful business is having a good team. He knew that a supermarket couldn't run smoothly without hard-working, dedicated employees. Juan made sure to hire people who shared his values and vision for the store. He offered his employees good wages and benefits, which helped them stay motivated and committed to their work.

One of the most important things Juan learned early on was that a business needs to be flexible. The world of retail is always changing, and Juan knew that he needed to adapt to those changes if he wanted to succeed. For example, when he saw that people were using credit cards more and more, he made sure to introduce credit card payments in his stores. Similarly, as technology improved, Juan introduced new systems to make the stores run more efficiently. This allowed his business to keep up with the times and continue growing.

Another valuable lesson Juan learned was the importance of planning for the future. When he first started turning the butcher shops into supermarkets, he didn't just think about the present; he thought about where the business would be in five, ten, and even twenty years. He understood that a business could only grow if it was carefully planned. Juan always made sure to look ahead and think about what the next steps would be.

Juan also learned that consistency is key in business. He knew that in order to build trust with customers, he had to make sure that his stores always offered good products and good service. People needed to know that when they came to his supermarket, they could expect the same level of quality and service every time. This consistency became a trademark of his business, and it helped to create loyal customers who kept coming back.

Finally, Juan learned that innovation is essential for success. He was always looking for ways to improve his stores and make them better. Whether it was by adding new products, introducing new technology, or improving the shopping experience, Juan was constantly looking for new ways to stay ahead of the competition.

The Importance of Customer Service

One of the key elements of Juan's early business strategy was customer service. Juan believed that a store should not only sell products but also provide a positive experience for its customers. He made sure that the employees were trained to be friendly and helpful. Juan also believed that a happy customer was a returning customer. He focused on making sure that his customers felt valued and appreciated. This focus on customer service became one of the reasons why his stores were so successful.

Juan's early experience with running his family's shops and turning them into supermarkets taught him many valuable lessons. He learned the importance of understanding customers' needs, building a strong team, planning for the future, being flexible, and maintaining consistency. These lessons would guide him as he went on to build one of the most successful supermarket chains in Spain, Mercadona. Each decision he made during these early years played a part in shaping the future of his business and setting the foundation for his long-term success.

In the next chapter, we will explore how Juan Roig expanded his business further and built Mercadona into the retail giant that it is today.

This chapter covers the key steps Juan Roig took to transition his family's butcher shops into a successful supermarket chain, highlighting the lessons he learned and the importance of customer service, team building, and future planning. The writing is designed to be clear and easy to understand for readers of all ages. Let me know if you'd like to modify anything further!

Chapter 3: The Birth of Mercadona

Why Juan Started Mercadona

In the early 1980s, Juan Roig realized that his family's business, which was mainly focused on butcher shops, was not going to be enough for the future. He saw how the grocery market in Spain was changing. Customers were looking for convenience, variety, and lower prices, but the small shops he managed couldn't offer those things. At the same time, larger supermarkets were starting to grow in other parts of the world, and Juan knew that it was time for a new idea.

Juan wanted to create something different—something that would meet the needs of the everyday shopper. He decided to create Mercadona, a supermarket chain that would stand out in the market. He believed that if he could combine a great shopping experience with affordable prices and a wide selection of quality products, people would be eager to shop there.

The name "Mercadona" came from the Spanish word for "market" and "home." Juan wanted people to feel like they were coming home when they visited his stores—comfortable, familiar, and ready to get everything they needed in one stop. The goal was simple: make shopping easy and enjoyable for everyone.

How Mercadona Was Different from Other Stores

When Mercadona first opened, it was different from the other stores around. Unlike the small, crowded shops that many people were used to, Mercadona offered a large, clean, and organized space where customers could find everything they needed. Juan's goal was to create a store where everything had its place and was easy to find. This was a big change for many shoppers, who were used to more traditional stores where products were not always neatly arranged.

One of the biggest differences was the layout of the stores. Instead of having lots of small aisles, Mercadona stores were designed to make shopping simple. They used wide aisles that allowed customers to move around freely and easily find the products they were looking for. Juan also made sure that products were placed in categories that made sense. For example, all the bread, milk, and dairy products were placed in one section, while all the cleaning supplies were in another. This was much more convenient for customers and helped them save time while shopping.

Another difference was the focus on everyday products. While other stores might focus on expensive luxury items, Juan wanted Mercadona to be a place where people could buy the things they needed for everyday life at affordable prices. He understood that most people didn't want to spend too much on groceries, so he made sure to offer high-quality products at low prices. This helped Mercadona attract a wide range of customers, from families to individuals, all looking for the best value.

Mercadona also introduced the idea of private-label products. These are products made specifically for a store, rather than from well-known brands. By offering private-label items, Mercadona could control the quality and pricing of the products, making sure they met the store's standards while also offering a better deal for customers. This was a major advantage over other supermarkets, where the prices of branded products were often higher.

The Focus on Customer Needs and Quality Products

One of the main reasons for Mercadona's success was Juan Roig's focus on understanding and meeting the needs of customers. From the very beginning, he made sure to listen to shoppers and learn what they wanted. Juan believed that the key to running a successful business was offering exactly what customers needed and making sure they were satisfied with every visit.

Mercadona placed a strong emphasis on quality. Juan didn't just want to offer cheap products; he wanted to offer products that were both affordable and high in quality. He made sure that all the items sold in Mercadona stores met strict quality standards. Whether it was fresh produce, dairy products, or frozen food, customers could trust that they were getting good value for their money.

To ensure that Mercadona was always offering the best products, Juan created a system of constant improvement. He worked closely with suppliers to find the best possible products and developed strict rules for quality control. Juan also encouraged his staff to keep an eye on product quality, making sure everything that went onto the shelves met the store's high standards.

Another important part of Mercadona's focus on customer needs was the store's customer service. Juan made sure that all employees were trained to be friendly and helpful, ensuring that customers always felt welcome when they walked into the store. This was important because Juan believed that good customer service was just as important as good products. He wanted customers to feel like they were getting more than just groceries; they were getting a pleasant shopping experience.

Juan also understood that convenience was key. He knew that many people didn't have time to spend hours shopping for groceries. That's why he focused on creating a store that was easy to navigate, quick to shop in, and always well-stocked with the most popular products. Mercadona's stores became known for being reliable and efficient, making them a go-to place for busy shoppers.

The Early Years: Challenges and Successes

The early years of Mercadona were not without challenges. Starting a new supermarket chain was difficult, and Juan faced many obstacles as he worked to build the business. One of the biggest challenges was convincing customers to trust a new store. At the time, Spain already had many well-established supermarkets, and it wasn't easy to convince people to switch to Mercadona.

But Juan was determined. He knew that once customers tried Mercadona, they would see the difference. To attract shoppers, he focused on offering the best quality products at the best prices. He also made sure the stores were always clean, well-organized, and easy to shop in. Slowly but surely, word started to spread, and more and more people began to visit Mercadona.

One of the key factors in Mercadona's early success was Juan's focus on innovation. While other supermarkets were still using old methods, Juan was always looking for ways to improve the shopping experience. For example, he introduced new technology to make the stores more efficient and used data to understand shopping patterns and improve product selection. This helped Mercadona stay ahead of the competition and provide the best possible service to its customers.

Another challenge was managing the rapid growth of Mercadona. As the store became more popular, Juan had to figure out how to expand the business without losing the quality and service that made it successful. To do this, he worked hard to create systems that could support the growth of the business. He hired a strong team of employees who shared his vision and values, and he invested in training programs to make sure everyone was on the same page.

Despite these challenges, Mercadona continued to grow. By the end of the 1990s, it had become one of the largest supermarket chains in Spain. The focus on quality products, affordable prices, and excellent customer service had paid off. Mercadona's success was proof that Juan

Roig's vision of a supermarket that prioritized the needs of customers could work.

The early years of Mercadona were full of obstacles, but through hard work, innovation, and a focus on customer satisfaction, Juan Roig was able to turn his dream into reality. Mercadona's growth and success set the stage for the company to become one of Spain's most beloved and successful supermarket chains.

This chapter covers the birth of Mercadona, from Juan Roig's decision to create a new supermarket chain to the challenges and successes of the early years. It emphasizes how the store's focus on customer needs, quality products, and innovation helped it stand out from the competition and eventually grow into a retail giant. Let me know if you'd like further adjustments!

Chapter 4: Juan's Investment Philosophy

What Does "Investment" Mean to Juan?

When we think about investing, we often think of putting money into something in the hope that it will grow over time. For Juan Roig, investment means much more than just putting money in stocks or companies. To Juan, investment is about creating long-lasting value. It is about finding ways to grow businesses in a way that will benefit everyone—customers, employees, and even the community.

Juan does not just want to make money quickly. His investment philosophy is about making decisions that will lead to steady growth in the long run. For him, this means investing in businesses that have strong potential for growth and that can improve the lives of the people who interact with them. Whether it's through opening new stores, improving products, or using better technology, Juan's idea of investment is always focused on the future and creating lasting success.

To Juan, good investment is about careful planning and patience. It's about understanding the risks and being ready to make decisions that will pay off over time. For him, the goal is to build something that can grow and last, rather than something that might give quick rewards but fail in the long term. Juan believes that the best investments are those that will continue to grow and provide value for many years, not just for a short time.

How He Decides Where to Put His Money

Juan Roig is very careful about where he puts his money. He does not invest in just any business or opportunity that comes his way. Instead, he focuses on businesses and projects that align with his values and his long-term vision for growth. He looks for companies and ideas that can be successful over time, ones that have the potential to make a difference in people's lives.

Before deciding where to invest, Juan takes the time to learn as much as he can about the business. He looks at its history, its people, its products, and its plans for the future. He wants to be sure that the company has a clear plan and a good strategy to succeed in the long run. This means he does not just invest in businesses that look good on the surface. He digs deep to understand how they work and whether they can continue growing and improving.

Juan also focuses on companies that have the ability to innovate. He believes that the future belongs to businesses that are willing to adapt and change with the times. He looks for companies that are not afraid to invest in new technologies or try new ways of doing things. This can include anything from using new machines to improving how products are made, to creating better ways of serving customers. For Juan, innovation is one of the key factors that can make a business successful in the long term.

Juan also pays attention to the people who run the businesses he invests in. He believes that strong leadership is critical to the success of any company. He looks for companies that have leaders who are passionate, smart, and dedicated to their work. Juan knows that having the right people in charge can make a huge difference in how a company performs, so he always considers the strength of the leadership team before making an investment.

Why Long-Term Growth Matters More Than Quick Profit

For Juan Roig, building a business is not about making a lot of money right away. He is not interested in short-term profits. Instead, he cares about long-term growth. He believes that businesses that focus on long-term success will always be more stable and successful in the end.

Juan understands that building something meaningful takes time. He knows that businesses need to grow slowly and steadily to avoid making risky moves that could hurt them later. By focusing on long-term growth, Juan is able to make smarter decisions that will lead to better results over the years. He is patient and willing to wait for investments to pay off, because he knows that true success takes time to build.

One of the reasons why long-term growth is so important to Juan is that it creates a strong foundation for the future. When a business grows slowly and carefully, it is better able to handle challenges and changes in the market. For example, if a business is focused on fast profits, it may take big risks and make decisions that could hurt the company in the long run. On the other hand, a company that focuses on steady growth is more likely to make wise choices and avoid dangerous risks.

Long-term growth also helps a business build loyalty with its customers. When customers see that a company is dedicated to quality, reliability, and improvement over time, they are more likely to stay loyal to that company. This kind of loyalty is important because it leads to repeat customers, positive reviews, and a solid reputation. For Juan, these factors are essential to building a successful business that can continue to grow for many years.

The Importance of Innovation and Technology in Business

Juan Roig is a big believer in the power of innovation and technology. He knows that in today's world, businesses must be willing to change and adapt to new technologies in order to stay competitive. For him, innovation is not just about creating new products, but about improving the way things are done in every part of the business.

In the case of Mercadona, Juan embraced technology from the very beginning. He understood that technology could make the shopping experience more efficient and could help the company grow faster. For example, he invested in new technology for managing inventory, so that Mercadona could keep track of products and make sure shelves were always stocked with the right items. This helped Mercadona avoid running out of popular products and allowed the stores to operate more smoothly.

Juan also believed that technology could improve the way Mercadona connected with its customers. He encouraged the company to develop better ways of gathering customer feedback and using that information to improve the shopping experience. Whether it was through using online surveys or improving customer service, Juan knew that technology could help Mercadona meet customer needs more effectively.

Innovation is also important to Juan because it allows businesses to stay ahead of the competition. In the retail industry, things change quickly. New products, new trends, and new technologies are always emerging. To stay successful, a company must be willing to innovate and try new things. Juan is always looking for ways to make Mercadona better, whether it's through new store designs, better product selection, or improved customer service.

For Juan, technology and innovation are not just nice additions to a business—they are necessary for long-term success. By staying focused on these areas, he believes that any business can continue to grow and thrive, even in a constantly changing world.

In this chapter, we explored Juan Roig's investment philosophy, which focuses on long-term growth, careful decision-making, and a commitment to innovation and technology. His approach to investing is grounded in a deep understanding of the businesses he supports and a clear vision for their future success. By focusing on these principles, Juan has been able to build and sustain one of Spain's most successful supermarket chains, Mercadona. Let me know if you need further changes or adjustments!

Chapter 5: Smart Business Decisions That Made Mercadona a Success

Choosing the Right Products to Sell

One of the key reasons why Mercadona became so successful is because Juan Roig made smart choices about the products the store sold. From the beginning, Juan understood that in order to stand out in the market, Mercadona needed to offer products that customers wanted and needed. He didn't just focus on popular brands; he made sure the products were high quality and met the needs of the people shopping in his stores.

Juan was very careful when selecting products. He wanted to sell items that were not only good but also affordable for his customers. He realized that many supermarkets focused on selling a lot of different products without thinking much about quality. Instead of filling his shelves with too many items, Juan decided to focus on the most important products that people needed every day, like fresh food, cleaning supplies, and basic household items. This simple approach made shopping at Mercadona easier and less overwhelming for customers.

Juan also paid attention to customer feedback. He listened to what people wanted and made sure to bring in products that matched their tastes. For example, if customers asked for better-tasting bread or a healthier type of milk, Mercadona would work on finding the right product to meet that need. By focusing on what customers cared about, Mercadona created a loyal customer base that trusted the store for its quality and thoughtful product selection.

Another key aspect of choosing the right products was Mercadona's commitment to having its own private label. Juan Roig realized that creating Mercadona's own brand of products could give the store better control over quality and pricing. Private label products are items that are sold under a store's own brand name instead of a well-known brand name. This allowed Mercadona to offer high-quality products at lower prices. Customers trusted these products because they were consistent in quality and often cheaper than national brands.

How Mercadona Stayed Ahead of Other Stores

Mercadona stayed ahead of its competitors by always thinking one step ahead. Juan Roig was never satisfied with just being good enough; he wanted Mercadona to be the best. One way he did this was by always adapting to changes in the market. He kept an eye on the latest trends and looked for new ways to improve Mercadona's offerings.

For example, Juan understood that customers were increasingly interested in convenience. They wanted shopping to be easier, faster, and more efficient. To meet this need, he invested in new store designs that made shopping more comfortable. Mercadona's stores are spacious, well-organized, and easy to navigate, so customers can find what they need quickly. This was a big improvement compared to many other stores that had crowded aisles and disorganized shelves.

Juan also made sure that Mercadona offered products that were not always available in other stores. He introduced unique items that attracted shoppers looking for something different. This made Mercadona stand out and attracted new customers who wanted to try something new. The store didn't just follow trends; it created its own way of doing things that made it unique in the retail world.

Another smart decision that helped Mercadona stay ahead of other stores was its focus on customer service. Juan believed that treating customers well was the key to keeping them coming back. Mercadona employees are trained to be friendly and helpful, and the stores are designed to be easy to shop in. Customers feel welcome and valued, and this made them more likely to return and recommend the store to others. Good customer service is something that many other stores overlook, but Mercadona made it a top priority.

Keeping Prices Low Without Losing Quality
One of the biggest challenges in running a successful business is keeping prices low while still offering high-quality products. Juan Roig understood that if Mercadona

wanted to grow, it had to offer affordable prices to attract customers. However, he didn't want to do this at the expense of quality.

Juan made sure that Mercadona kept costs low by focusing on efficiency. He carefully controlled how the store operated, looking for ways to cut waste and reduce unnecessary expenses. By running the stores efficiently, Mercadona was able to lower its prices without sacrificing quality.

Mercadona also built strong relationships with its suppliers. This allowed the company to get better prices for the products it bought. Juan worked directly with suppliers to ensure that Mercadona could offer the best deals while maintaining the quality that customers expected. Because Mercadona bought in large quantities, it could negotiate better prices and pass those savings on to customers.

At the same time, Juan was very particular about the quality of the products Mercadona sold. He did not allow the store to compromise on quality just to save money. For example, when Mercadona decided to introduce its own brand of products, it worked closely with experts to make sure that the products were as good as, or even better than, the national brands. This commitment to quality helped build trust with customers and made them feel confident in the store's products.

Why Juan Focused on Technology and Efficiency

Technology and efficiency played a huge role in the success of Mercadona. Juan Roig understood that in order to stay competitive, Mercadona needed to use the latest technology to improve its operations. He knew that technology could help make the store run more smoothly, lower costs, and provide a better experience for customers.

One of the ways Juan used technology was by implementing advanced systems for managing inventory. This allowed Mercadona to keep track of the products it sold and ensure that shelves were always stocked with the right items. By using technology to manage inventory, Mercadona was able to reduce waste and avoid running out of popular products. This improved efficiency and helped the store provide better service to customers.

Juan also focused on making Mercadona's supply chain more efficient. The supply chain is the system that brings products from suppliers to stores. Mercadona worked with suppliers to improve delivery times, reduce costs, and streamline the process. This allowed Mercadona to keep prices low and improve the speed at which products reached the stores.

Another important technology that Juan introduced was a customer feedback system. By gathering feedback from customers, Mercadona was able to make quick improvements to its products and services. This also helped the company stay ahead of customer needs and offer a better shopping experience.

Finally, Juan focused on making the shopping experience easier and faster for customers. Mercadona's stores were designed with the customer in mind. Juan used technology to make the checkout process quicker and more efficient, so customers didn't have to wait in long lines. This focus on technology helped Mercadona stay competitive with other stores and ensure that customers had a positive experience every time they visited.

In this chapter, we have learned how Juan Roig made smart business decisions that helped Mercadona become the success it is today. By choosing the right products, staying ahead of competitors, keeping prices low without sacrificing quality, and focusing on technology and efficiency, Mercadona was able to build a loyal customer base and grow rapidly. These smart decisions helped turn Mercadona into one of the largest and most successful supermarket chains in Spain.

Chapter 6: The Role of Employees in Mercadona's Growth

Treating Employees as Partners

Juan Roig, the founder of Mercadona, believed that employees were not just workers but partners in the business. He understood that if Mercadona was going to succeed, it had to have a team of people who were not just doing their jobs, but were deeply invested in the store's success. Juan treated his employees with respect and fairness, making sure that they felt like a part of the Mercadona family.

To create this environment, Juan Roig made sure to provide his employees with good working conditions. For example, he offered stable and secure jobs, and he worked to make sure the store was a place where employees could feel safe and comfortable. By treating employees as partners, Juan created a sense of loyalty among the workers. They didn't just see their job as a way to make money; they saw it as a shared goal of making Mercadona the best supermarket.

Juan also involved employees in important business decisions. He wanted their input on how to improve operations, products, and customer service. This made the workers feel valued and gave them a sense of ownership in the company's success.

When employees are treated as partners, they are more likely to go above and beyond to help the company grow, and this is exactly what happened at Mercadona.

Offering Full-Time Jobs for Everyone
One of the things that set Mercadona apart from other companies was its focus on offering full-time jobs to as many employees as possible. In many businesses, part-time jobs are common, but Juan Roig believed that offering full-time jobs was important for several reasons. Full-time work gives employees more stability in their lives. They know that they can count on a steady income and benefits, which helps them feel secure and focused on their work.

Mercadona became known for offering full-time jobs, even to entry-level workers. Juan Roig believed that when people have stable work, they are more likely to be loyal, dedicated, and motivated. Instead of having many part-time workers who might not stay with the company for long, Mercadona gave its employees long-term positions that they could count on. This also helped reduce turnover, which is when employees leave a company and need to be replaced. High turnover can be expensive for businesses, but by offering full-time jobs, Mercadona kept its team together for a long time, helping the company grow.

In addition to offering full-time jobs, Mercadona made sure that the jobs were well-paid and offered good benefits.

Employees received health insurance, retirement plans, and other benefits that made them feel valued and cared for. This commitment to offering good jobs helped Mercadona attract and keep talented employees who were dedicated to the company's success.

How Happy Employees Lead to a Better Business

Juan Roig understood that happy employees lead to a better business. He knew that when employees are treated well and feel happy at work, they are more productive and provide better service to customers. In a store like Mercadona, where customer service is very important, happy employees play a key role in making sure that customers have a great shopping experience.

When employees are satisfied with their jobs, they are more likely to help customers in a friendly and helpful way. This creates a positive environment in the store and makes customers feel welcome. Customers appreciate when employees are friendly and willing to assist them with finding products or answering questions. This helps create a strong relationship between the store and its customers, and it makes customers want to return.

Juan also recognized that happy employees are more likely to stay with the company and work hard. When people enjoy what they do and feel that they are part of something bigger than just a job, they are more motivated to do their best. This means that employees at Mercadona weren't just there to complete tasks; they were committed to doing great work because they cared about the success of the business.

Mercadona's focus on happy employees also helped the company become more efficient. When employees are satisfied, they are more likely to share ideas for improving how things are done in the store. These ideas can lead to better processes, lower costs, and improved customer service, all of which help the company grow and succeed.

Why Juan Believes in Teamwork and Loyalty

One of the main reasons Mercadona succeeded was because Juan Roig believed in the power of teamwork. He didn't just want people to work together; he wanted them to trust each other, communicate openly, and share ideas. Juan created a company culture where teamwork was encouraged, and employees were all working toward the same goal: making Mercadona the best supermarket.

Juan Roig also believed that loyalty was key to building a successful business. He understood that when employees are loyal to the company, they work harder, are more dedicated, and stay with the business for the long term. Mercadona's focus on loyalty meant that employees were not just working for their paycheck; they felt a deep connection to the company. This loyalty created a positive work environment, and it made employees feel proud of the work they were doing.

To build loyalty, Juan made sure that employees felt respected and valued. He gave them opportunities to grow within the company. Many of Mercadona's top managers started out as cashiers or stock clerks. Juan believed in promoting from within, and he made sure that employees had opportunities for advancement. This not only kept employees loyal to the company, but it also helped Mercadona build a strong leadership team from within.

In addition to loyalty among employees, Juan believed in building loyalty with customers. He knew that if employees were loyal to the company, they would treat customers with the same level of respect and care. Loyal employees are more likely to give their best effort, which directly impacts customer satisfaction. This helped Mercadona build a large, loyal customer base that trusted the store and returned to shop there regularly.

Training and Support for Employees
Juan Roig also invested heavily in training and supporting his employees. He knew that the more skilled and knowledgeable employees were, the better they could serve customers and help the business grow. Mercadona provided extensive training to its employees, ensuring that they understood the company's values, goals, and processes.

Mercadona also supported its employees in other ways. Juan Roig was always looking for ways to make employees' jobs easier and more enjoyable. For example, Mercadona introduced tools and technologies that helped employees perform their tasks more efficiently. This made their work less stressful and allowed them to focus on delivering great customer service.

In addition to training and technology, Juan ensured that employees had the support they needed to grow within the company. He encouraged open communication and made sure that employees felt comfortable sharing their thoughts and ideas. This created a work culture where employees felt supported, heard, and respected.

In this chapter, we have seen how Juan Roig's focus on employees helped Mercadona become one of the most successful supermarket chains in Spain. By treating employees as partners, offering full-time jobs, creating a happy work environment, and promoting teamwork and loyalty, Juan Roig built a strong foundation for Mercadona's success. Happy employees led to better service, higher productivity, and a loyal customer base, all of which contributed to the company's growth and success.

Chapter 7: Overcoming Challenges with Patience and Hard Work

The Difficult Times: How Juan Stayed Strong

Every business faces difficult times, and Juan Roig's journey with Mercadona was no exception. In the early years, there were many challenges that could have made Juan give up, but he didn't. Instead, he faced each problem with strength, patience, and determination.

One of the biggest difficulties was competing against other big supermarket chains. At the time, there were many well-established stores that were already popular with customers. Mercadona had to work hard to win customers and convince them to choose their stores. It was tough, but Juan didn't give up. He knew that patience was important. Instead of rushing into decisions, he took his time to understand the needs of his customers and how to meet those needs better than anyone else.

There were also financial challenges. Starting and growing a business costs money, and sometimes Mercadona did not have enough funds to do everything it wanted. But Juan stayed focused and made sure the money was spent wisely. He knew that the road to success would not be easy, but he was willing to work hard and stay patient. Juan understood that every business goes through hard times, and it was important to keep moving forward, even when things seemed tough.

Making Tough Decisions for the Future

As Mercadona grew, Juan Roig had to make many tough decisions to ensure the company's long-term success. One of the most important decisions was about how Mercadona would compete in the crowded supermarket market. Juan knew that Mercadona had to offer something different to stand out, so he focused on two things: customer service and quality.

One difficult decision Juan made was to only sell high-quality products, even if it meant higher prices at times. He wanted

Mercadona to be known for offering the best products, which meant that the company had to be selective about what it sold. This was a risky decision because other stores might have been selling cheaper products, but Juan knew that customers would appreciate the quality and would keep coming back.

Another important decision was about the technology Mercadona used. Juan believed that technology could help improve the way the company operated, but it required a large investment. This was a tough decision because it meant spending a lot of money upfront. However, Juan believed that the investment would pay off in the long run. He understood that staying ahead in the business world required using new tools and technologies, so he made the decision to invest in things like better computer systems, supply chain management, and in-store technology to make the shopping experience easier for customers.

Making these tough decisions was not always easy. It required careful thinking and planning. But Juan trusted in his vision for the company and made choices that he believed would help Mercadona grow into a successful business in the future.

Learning from Mistakes and Moving Forward

Like all successful business leaders, Juan Roig made mistakes along the way. But instead of seeing mistakes as failures, he saw them as learning opportunities. Juan understood that making mistakes was a part of growing a business. What mattered most was how he responded to those mistakes.

For example, early on, Juan learned that some of the products Mercadona sold were not what customers wanted. At first, Mercadona had too many different products on the shelves, and some were not selling well. This was a mistake because it meant Mercadona was wasting space and resources on products that customers didn't need. Instead of ignoring the problem, Juan took action. He carefully studied the products that sold the most and removed the ones that didn't perform well. By learning from this mistake, Mercadona was able to improve its product selection and make sure that only the best and most popular items were available to customers.

Another mistake Juan made was not always knowing the exact amount of stock that each store would need. Sometimes, there would be too many products in one store and not enough in another. This caused some stores to run out of popular items, which frustrated customers. Again, Juan didn't ignore the problem. He worked with his team to create a better inventory system. This helped ensure that each store had the right amount of products and customers could always find what they needed. Juan's ability to learn from these mistakes made Mercadona a better company.

Juan also understood that sometimes, even when things are going well, it is important to be humble and accept that there is always room for improvement. For example, when Mercadona first started, it was a smaller company, and there were fewer stores. Juan could have been proud of what he had built, but he knew there was more work to do. Instead of resting on his success, he kept looking for ways to make Mercadona better. He knew that no matter how successful a company becomes, it's important to continue learning and growing.

The Importance of Patience in Success
Patience was one of the most important qualities Juan Roig needed to develop as he built Mercadona. Growing a business takes time, and there are no shortcuts to success.

In the beginning, it seemed like the road ahead would be long and difficult, but Juan stayed patient. He knew that building a strong foundation would pay off in the future, even if the results weren't immediate.

Juan's patience paid off when Mercadona became more and more successful. His decision to focus on quality, customer service, and the right products started to show results. Customers began to trust Mercadona more, and the company slowly built a loyal customer base. Instead of rushing into quick decisions to make more money, Juan focused on the long-term growth of the business. This made all the difference. Mercadona became one of Spain's largest supermarket chains, with thousands of employees and loyal customers who valued its commitment to quality.

Juan also knew that growth doesn't happen overnight. Every step in the journey took time, and he had to be patient with the process. Whether it was improving the product selection, expanding the number of stores, or investing in technology, Juan stayed committed to his goals. He didn't give up, even when it was hard, and that patience was key to Mercadona's long-term success.

Staying Focused on the Big Picture
Throughout all the challenges, Juan Roig never lost sight of the big picture. He always kept his vision for Mercadona clear in his mind: to build a supermarket that provided

high-quality products, great customer service, and fair prices. Even when things didn't go as planned, Juan stayed focused on this vision and used every challenge as an opportunity to learn and improve.

By staying focused on the big picture, Juan made decisions that were best for the future of Mercadona, not just for the present. Every tough decision, every mistake, and every moment of patience helped shape Mercadona into the successful company it is today.

In this chapter, we have seen how Juan Roig overcame challenges with patience, hard work, and a focus on learning from mistakes. Whether dealing with tough times, making difficult decisions, or learning from errors, Juan's ability to stay strong and move forward was key to Mercadona's success. His patience and willingness to learn from mistakes helped build a company that would become one of Spain's largest and most successful supermarket chains.

Chapter 8: Juan Roig's Investment in Other Businesses

Expanding Beyond Mercadona: Investing in New Ideas

Juan Roig, known for his success with Mercadona, didn't stop there. Once he had built Mercadona into a powerful and trusted supermarket chain, he started looking for new opportunities to invest in. Juan understood that a great entrepreneur doesn't just stick to one thing; they explore other ideas and help grow new businesses.

After achieving success with Mercadona, Juan wanted to be part of projects that could bring about new ideas and innovations. He didn't just want to make money. He wanted to invest in businesses that could make a real difference and solve problems. To do this, he turned his attention to many different industries, not just supermarkets. Juan's philosophy was simple: invest in ideas that were new, creative, and could have a big impact on people's lives.

He began to look for businesses with potential for growth, just like he did with Mercadona when it was starting. Juan believed that great businesses could be built in any sector, not only in supermarkets. Whether it was technology, healthcare, or other services, he wanted to be involved in companies that were making things better and more efficient.

Juan started investing in smaller companies that were looking for support to grow. He used his knowledge and resources to help these businesses become successful, just like he had done with Mercadona. This showed that Juan believed in helping new ideas grow, even if they were outside of his original business.

How Juan Helps Other Entrepreneurs Grow

Juan Roig's approach to helping other entrepreneurs is one of the key reasons why he is such a respected businessman. Instead of just providing money and expecting quick returns, Juan works closely with the businesses he invests in. He offers advice, shares his experiences, and helps entrepreneurs make decisions that will lead to long-term success.

One of the ways Juan helps entrepreneurs is by offering them more than just financial support. He uses his deep understanding of business to guide them. Juan knows that running a business isn't just about having a good product; it's also about making smart decisions, building a strong team, and managing resources well. He shares this knowledge with the businesses he supports to make sure they are set up for success.

Juan also encourages entrepreneurs to focus on innovation. He believes that to stay ahead in business, companies must continuously improve and find new ways to solve problems. This is something he applied to Mercadona, and he expects the same from the businesses he invests in. By investing in creative and forward-thinking companies, Juan helps them grow and succeed in competitive markets.

Another way Juan helps entrepreneurs is by promoting a culture of teamwork and trust. He believes that a successful business isn't built on one person's efforts but on the collaboration of many. He encourages entrepreneurs to build strong teams that work well together and support each other's ideas. This focus on teamwork is something Juan values deeply, and it is a central part of how he invests in other businesses.

What Makes His Investments Different from Others?

Juan Roig's approach to investing is different from many other investors. While other investors might focus only on making quick profits, Juan looks for long-term success. He invests in businesses because he believes in them and wants to see them grow. His focus is not just on making money quickly but on helping businesses become stronger over time.

One of the key differences in Juan's investments is that he doesn't just want to make a profit. He wants to create value for everyone involved—employees, customers, and the community. When Juan invests in a company, he looks at how that business can improve the world in some way. He wants to invest in businesses that will make a difference in people's lives, whether through better products, new services, or innovative ideas.

Another unique aspect of Juan's investment style is that he takes an active role in the companies he invests in. Unlike many investors who may provide funding and then step back, Juan likes to stay involved. He works with the entrepreneurs, providing them with guidance and helping them solve problems as they arise. His hands-on approach ensures that he can help the businesses he invests in reach their full potential. Juan's experience in growing Mercadona means that he has valuable insights to share, and he is always willing to help others succeed.

Juan also focuses on long-term growth, rather than chasing quick profits. Many investors may look for businesses that will provide immediate returns, but Juan looks for companies that can keep growing and improving over many years. He understands that business success doesn't happen overnight. That's why he is willing to invest in companies that may take time to grow but have the potential to achieve great things in the future.

Juan's commitment to quality is another reason his investments are different. Just like Mercadona, he looks for companies that are focused on providing high-quality products or services. Juan knows that quality matters to customers, and he wants to support businesses that are dedicated to offering the best. Whether it's in technology, healthcare, or retail, Juan's investments are always made with a focus on excellence.

Finally, Juan is known for his ability to spot potential in businesses that others might overlook. He doesn't just invest in popular industries or follow the latest trends. Instead, he looks for businesses that have the potential to change the market in some way. This means he often invests in innovative startups or smaller companies that others may not have considered. Juan's ability to see opportunities where others might not is what makes his investments so special.

Juan's Legacy as an Investor

Juan Roig's investments have not only helped him expand his own business empire, but they have also helped other entrepreneurs succeed. By investing in companies that focus on innovation, quality, and long-term growth, Juan has played a role in shaping many industries in Spain. His approach to investing has set him apart as a businessman who cares about the future and the people behind the companies he supports.

As a result, Juan Roig's legacy as an investor is one of creating value, supporting new ideas, and helping businesses grow in ways that benefit society. His commitment to innovation, quality, and long-term success has made a lasting impact on the Spanish business world.

In conclusion, Juan Roig's investments in other businesses reflect his belief in the power of new ideas and the importance of long-term success. By focusing on companies that can grow and make a real difference, he has helped many entrepreneurs achieve their goals. His approach to investing is unique because it combines financial support with hands-on guidance, teamwork, and a focus on quality. This philosophy has made Juan a respected figure in the business world, and his investments continue to shape industries and create lasting value.

Chapter 9: The Legacy of Juan Roig Alfonso

The Impact of Mercadona on Spain and Beyond

Juan Roig Alfonso's legacy is mostly defined by his creation and leadership of Mercadona, one of Spain's largest and most successful supermarket chains. When Juan started Mercadona, he had a simple but powerful idea: offer high-quality products at fair prices while always thinking about the customer. This idea quickly turned Mercadona into more than just a supermarket; it became a leader in the Spanish retail market and an example for many businesses.

Mercadona changed how people shop in Spain. Before Mercadona, many supermarkets didn't focus on customer service in the same way. They had products, but they didn't always care much about what the customers needed or wanted. Juan Roig focused on creating an experience where customers felt important. This shift in focus transformed Mercadona into a go-to place for people to shop for food and other products.

Beyond Spain, the impact of Mercadona has been noticed by other countries as well. Its focus on customer satisfaction, product quality, and affordable prices has made it a model for supermarkets worldwide. Mercadona's success story has been an inspiration for many businesses outside of

Spain, teaching others how to build a customer-first company. Juan's vision and his ability to stick to his core values even in challenging times have set an example for businesses in other countries, proving that with patience, commitment, and a clear purpose, success is achievable.

How Juan's Investments Have Changed the Retail World

Juan Roig didn't stop with Mercadona; he also invested in other businesses and projects that have changed the way people view retail. His approach to business, which combines innovation, teamwork, and quality, has had a significant impact on the retail world, both in Spain and globally.

One of the main ways Juan has changed the retail world is by focusing on efficiency. He has always believed that a well-run company can offer good prices while still maintaining high standards. For example, Mercadona's supply chain is highly efficient, meaning the company can reduce costs and pass those savings on to customers without sacrificing product quality. This approach has forced other retailers to rethink their business strategies, inspiring them to be more efficient in their operations.

In addition to efficiency, Juan has also pushed for greater investment in technology. From the very beginning, he recognized the importance of technology in business. Whether it was using computers to track inventory or adopting new systems to improve logistics, technology has been a key part of Mercadona's success. Juan's ability to see the potential of technology early on has made Mercadona a leader in using technology to improve business operations. As other companies have followed his example, Juan's influence has helped the entire retail sector become more modern and efficient.

Juan's investments in other industries also reflect his belief in innovation. He doesn't just invest in retail; he looks for opportunities in other areas that can benefit from his business approach. His focus on quality, customer service, and long-term growth has impacted not just supermarkets but a wide range of industries. By helping small businesses and startups grow, Juan is shaping the future of many sectors, making them more customer-focused and efficient.

What Juan Wants His Business to Teach Others

Juan Roig's legacy is not just about building a successful business; it is also about teaching others how to succeed in business. He believes that every business should have clear values and principles, and that by sticking to these principles, success can be achieved.

One of the most important lessons Juan wants to teach others is the importance of customer satisfaction. From the beginning, Mercadona was built around the idea of always putting customers first. Juan has always said that businesses should focus on the needs and wants of their customers above all else. By giving people what they want—good products at fair prices—businesses can build strong, long-lasting relationships with their customers.

Juan also teaches the value of hard work and patience. He knows that success doesn't happen overnight, and he believes that building a business takes time and effort. He teaches that, even during difficult times, it is important to stay focused and keep working toward long-term goals. Juan's journey with Mercadona has shown that sticking to your principles, working hard, and being patient can lead to big rewards, even when the road ahead looks tough.

Teamwork is another important lesson that Juan wants to teach. In Mercadona, he has always treated employees like partners, working together to achieve common goals. Juan knows that a business can only be successful if everyone works together, and he believes that a strong, loyal team is one of the keys to success. By encouraging teamwork and treating employees well, Juan has built a business culture that values trust and collaboration. This philosophy has had a positive impact on Mercadona's growth, and it serves as a valuable lesson for businesses everywhere.

Juan also believes in the power of innovation. Throughout his career, he has always looked for ways to improve, whether by introducing new products, finding more efficient ways to operate, or using technology to enhance the customer experience. Juan shows that, in business, it is important to never stop looking for ways to grow and improve. He believes that innovation is what keeps businesses competitive and able to meet the changing needs of customers.

Finally, Juan's legacy teaches the importance of making decisions that benefit the long-term health of the business, rather than just focusing on quick profits. Throughout his career, he has made decisions that prioritize long-term growth over short-term gains. For example, his focus on quality products and customer service might have cost more at first, but it has led to lasting success for Mercadona.

Juan's emphasis on long-term goals has helped him create a business that not only survives but thrives in a competitive market.

Juan Roig's Personal Influence on Spanish Business Culture

Juan Roig's influence extends beyond just Mercadona and his investments. His approach to business has had a lasting impact on Spanish business culture. Juan has shown that it is possible to run a business with a clear set of values and principles, even in challenging times. He has helped change the way people in Spain think about entrepreneurship and success.

His commitment to quality, customer satisfaction, and long-term growth has encouraged many young entrepreneurs in Spain to think differently about business. Instead of focusing only on making money, Juan has shown that it is possible to create a successful business while also improving the lives of customers, employees, and communities. This shift in mindset has helped create a new generation of entrepreneurs who value the long-term impact of their businesses.

Juan's legacy is also evident in the success of the companies he has helped grow and support. Through his investments and partnerships, he has helped create many businesses that are making a positive difference in Spain and beyond. His focus on teamwork, efficiency, and innovation has inspired these companies to adopt the same values, further extending his influence across many sectors.

Conclusion

Juan Roig's legacy is a testament to the power of customer-focused businesses, hard work, and innovation. Through Mercadona, he changed the retail landscape in Spain and beyond, showing that it is possible to build a successful business while staying true to core values. His investments in other businesses and his influence on Spanish business culture have left a lasting impact, teaching others the importance of quality, teamwork, and long-term growth.

Juan's business philosophy is a blueprint for future entrepreneurs, proving that with patience, dedication, and a focus on innovation, it is possible to build a business that not only succeeds but also makes a positive impact on the world. His legacy continues to inspire and teach others how to create businesses that prioritize customers, employees, and sustainable growth.

Chapter 10: What We Can Learn from Juan Roig's Success

Juan Roig's journey with Mercadona offers valuable lessons for anyone who wants to build a successful business, invest wisely, and make a positive impact on the world. By focusing on certain key principles, he turned Mercadona into one of the largest supermarket chains in Spain, while also influencing the way people think about business and investment. In this chapter, we'll explore the important lessons we can learn from Juan Roig's success and how you can apply them to your own life.

Key Lessons in Business and Investing

Juan Roig's success didn't come by chance. He followed a set of key principles that guided his decisions, and these lessons can help anyone achieve success in business or investment. Here are some of the most important lessons we can learn from him:

1. Focus on Quality and Customer Satisfaction

One of the main reasons for Mercadona's success is its focus on quality products and customer satisfaction. From the very beginning, Juan Roig made sure that customers could rely on Mercadona for good quality at fair prices. Instead of cutting corners or focusing only on profits, he believed that when customers are happy with the products and services, they will return and recommend the store to others. This simple yet powerful focus on quality has helped Mercadona build strong customer loyalty.

Lesson: In business, always prioritize the needs and satisfaction of your customers. When you take care of your customers, they will keep coming back, and your business will grow.

2. Invest in Efficiency

Another important lesson is the focus on efficiency. Juan Roig understood that running a business efficiently means reducing waste and costs. At Mercadona, he implemented systems that helped streamline operations, making the store run smoothly and keeping prices low for customers. He used technology to track inventory, manage supply chains, and improve the way products were delivered to the stores. This focus on efficiency not only helped Mercadona save money, but it also improved the shopping experience for customers.

Lesson: Being efficient is key to any business. Use technology and smart systems to improve your operations, save time, and reduce costs. This will help you run a successful business that can compete in the market.

3. Think Long-Term, Not Just Short-Term

Juan Roig is known for thinking about the future, not just the present. While many companies focus on making quick profits, Juan has always focused on building a strong, sustainable business. He didn't make decisions just for short-term gain. Instead, he thought about what would be best for the company in the long run. Whether it was investing in employee training, improving product quality, or expanding the store network, Juan was always focused on long-term growth.

Lesson: Don't be tempted to chase short-term profits. Instead, focus on building a business that will thrive in the long run. Think about where you want to be in the next 5, 10, or 20 years and make decisions that will help you reach those goals.

4. Empower Employees and Build a Strong Team

One of Juan's core beliefs is that employees should be treated like partners. He valued teamwork and created a company culture where employees felt supported and important. Juan knew that a happy and motivated team would work harder and perform better. At Mercadona, employees were given opportunities for training and development, and many were promoted from within the company. This approach helped Mercadona grow while creating a loyal and committed workforce.

Lesson: Treat your employees well. Empower them, invest in their growth, and build a strong, loyal team. A motivated and well-trained team is crucial to the success of any business.

5. Invest Wisely and Think About the Future

Juan Roig is also known for his smart investments. Beyond Mercadona, he has invested in other businesses and startups that align with his values and long-term goals. Instead of making quick investments in trendy businesses, he focuses on opportunities that have the potential for sustainable growth. His ability to spot good investment opportunities and support other entrepreneurs has helped him create a strong network of successful businesses.

Lesson: When investing, think carefully about the long-term potential. Look for businesses that have solid foundations and room to grow. Don't focus on making quick profits; instead, aim to build something that will last.

How You Can Apply His Strategies to Your Own Life

Juan Roig's strategies are not just for big businesses or investors. You can apply these principles to your own life, no matter what goals you have. Here's how you can take these lessons and use them to achieve success:

1. Focus on Quality in Everything You Do

Whether you are working on a school project, starting a small business, or pursuing a career, focusing on quality is always important. Just like Juan Roig focused on high-quality products at Mercadona, you should aim to do your best in whatever you take on. People will notice when you put effort into your work, and they will respect you for it.

2. Be Efficient and Use Your Time Wisely

Time is one of our most valuable resources. Juan Roig's focus on efficiency shows that using time wisely is key to success. Whether you're studying, working, or managing a project, finding ways to be more efficient can help you achieve your goals faster. Use tools and systems that help you stay organized, manage tasks, and avoid wasting time on things that don't matter.

3. Think About the Future

Juan Roig teaches us the value of thinking long-term. Instead of making decisions based on what will give you the quickest reward, focus on what will help you achieve your goals in the future. This might mean saving money, learning new skills, or building relationships that will help you in the long run. When you think about the future, you can make smarter decisions today that will lead to greater success tomorrow.

4. Work Well With Others

In any area of life, it's important to build good relationships and work well with others. Whether it's at school, in your family, or at work, teamwork and cooperation will help you reach your goals.

Just like Juan Roig built a strong team at Mercadona, you should focus on working with others who can help you grow and succeed. Support others, and they will support you.

5. Be Patient and Stay Committed

Success doesn't happen overnight. Juan Roig's journey with Mercadona shows that staying committed to your goals, even when things are tough, will lead to long-term rewards. Don't give up if things don't go as planned. Keep working hard, learning from mistakes, and making adjustments along the way. With patience and persistence, you will eventually see the results of your efforts.

The Power of Thinking Long-Term and Staying Committed

One of the biggest lessons from Juan Roig's success is the power of thinking long-term. In a world where many people focus on quick results, Juan Roig's commitment to building a strong, sustainable business has proven that taking the long view pays off. Whether you're building a career, growing a business, or working on a personal goal, thinking long-term can help you stay focused and motivated, even when challenges arise.

Staying committed to your goals, even when progress seems slow, is also important. Juan Roig's ability to stay patient and dedicated to his vision is a powerful reminder that success is often a marathon, not a sprint. By sticking to your plans and working hard every day, you can achieve great things over time.

Conclusion

Juan Roig's success with Mercadona offers valuable lessons for anyone who wants to achieve great things in business and life. By focusing on quality, efficiency, long-term goals, teamwork, and smart investments, Juan has built a legacy that continues to inspire others. You can apply these principles to your own life, no matter what your goals are. Whether you're starting a business, pursuing a career, or just trying to improve yourself, the lessons from Juan Roig's success can help you achieve your dreams. Stay committed, think long-term, and always strive for excellence—these are the keys to success.

Conclusion

Juan Roig Alfonso is a businessman whose journey has shaped the way people think about success, business, and investing. His story is one of hard work, smart decisions, and a deep understanding of what it takes to create something that lasts. As we reflect on Juan Roig's path, we can learn many lessons that will help us in our own lives, whether in business, investment, or personal goals. This chapter will look back at his journey, the future of his business, and why Juan Roig is a business role model for everyone.

Reflecting on Juan Roig Alfonso's Journey

Juan Roig's journey to success started with his involvement in his family's business, but his determination and vision took him much further. He is best known for turning Mercadona, a small family-run store, into one of the largest supermarket chains in Spain. This journey wasn't easy, and it took years of hard work, careful planning, and making the right decisions at the right time.

What makes Juan Roig's story special is his focus on doing things the right way. Instead of looking for quick wins, he worked hard to build a business that would last for generations. He didn't just want to make money. He wanted to build something that people would trust and rely on. His approach to business is a great example of how patience, dedication, and focusing on quality can lead to success.

As we look back on his journey, we can see the importance of sticking to one's values, working hard, and always aiming for improvement. Juan Roig faced challenges along the way, but he never gave up. Instead, he learned from each obstacle and used it to grow stronger and smarter. This attitude has made him a true leader in the business world, and his story is a reminder that success doesn't happen overnight. It takes time, effort, and a commitment to doing things right.

The Future of Mercadona and His Investments

Juan Roig has already made a huge impact with Mercadona, but his journey is far from over. The future of Mercadona looks bright, as the company continues to grow and expand. Juan Roig has always focused on innovation, and it's clear that he will keep pushing the company forward with new ideas and improvements. Mercadona's commitment to quality products, customer service, and efficiency will ensure that it stays a top player in the retail industry for years to come.

Beyond Mercadona, Juan Roig has invested in many other businesses and startups, showing that he is not afraid to take risks and explore new opportunities. His investments are not just about making money; they are about supporting businesses that have the potential to grow and make a positive impact. Juan Roig believes in helping others succeed, and his investments reflect that belief. As he continues to invest in new ideas, we can expect to see more successful businesses emerge from his support.

The future of Juan Roig's investments is exciting because he has a keen eye for spotting potential. Whether it's in retail, technology, or other industries, Juan knows how to find opportunities that align with his values and long-term goals. This means that, just like Mercadona, the businesses he invests in will continue to grow and make a difference in the world.

What Makes Juan Roig a Business Role Model for Everyone

There are many reasons why Juan Roig is a role model for anyone interested in business. One of the main reasons is his approach to success. He didn't try to follow the latest trends or make quick profits. Instead, he built Mercadona on a solid foundation of values, hard work, and a commitment to quality. This long-term thinking is what has made him stand out in the business world. He didn't just focus on immediate results; he thought about the future and worked towards creating something that would last.

Another reason Juan Roig is a great role model is his focus on efficiency. In business, time and resources are precious. Juan Roig's ability to streamline operations, reduce waste, and make the most of what he has is something that everyone can learn from. Whether you're running a big business or working on a small project, being efficient helps you achieve more with less effort.

Juan Roig is also a role model because of his leadership. He knows that a business can't succeed without a strong team. His focus on empowering employees, building a positive company culture, and investing in the growth of others has helped Mercadona become one of the most successful companies in Spain. He treats his employees like partners, which motivates them to work harder and be more committed to the company's goals.

His approach to investment also sets him apart from many other business leaders. Juan Roig doesn't just look for opportunities to make money. He looks for businesses that align with his values and have the potential to grow in the long term. His investments are not just about profit; they're about supporting businesses that can make a difference in the world. This mindset shows that business success can be about more than just money; it can be about making a positive impact.

Finally, Juan Roig is a role model because of his ability to stay committed. His journey to success wasn't quick or easy, but he stayed focused on his goals and kept working toward them. He teaches us that perseverance is key. No matter how difficult things get, it's important to stay committed and keep working toward your goals. Success doesn't come overnight, but with hard work and patience, it is achievable.

What We Can Learn from Juan Roig

Juan Roig's story offers many important lessons for anyone looking to achieve success, whether in business, investing, or other areas of life. Here are a few key takeaways:

1. Think Long-Term: Juan Roig's success wasn't about making quick profits. He focused on building a business that would

last. Thinking about the future and making decisions that will benefit you in the long run is key to achieving lasting success.

2. Work Hard and Stay Committed: Success takes time and effort. Juan Roig shows us that even when things get tough, staying committed to your goals will eventually lead to success.

3. Invest in What You Believe In: Juan Roig's investments are focused on businesses that align with his values. He teaches us the importance of investing in things that have the potential to grow and make a positive impact.

4. Empower Your Team: A business can't succeed without a strong, motivated team.

Juan Roig's leadership shows the power of empowering others, treating them with respect, and helping them grow.

5. Focus on Quality: Whether it's a product, service, or idea, focusing on quality is always important. When you provide quality, people will trust you and come back for more.

Conclusion

Juan Roig Alfonso is a business leader whose journey has left a lasting impact on the world. His success with Mercadona and his smart investments have made him a role model for anyone who wants to build something meaningful and lasting. By thinking long-term, working hard, empowering others, and focusing on quality, Juan Roig has created a business legacy that will inspire future generations. His approach shows that success is not just about making money—it's about making a difference. Whether you're in business or any other area of life, there's a lot we can learn from Juan Roig's journey and the values that have guided him throughout his career.

www.ingramcontent.com/pod-product-compliance
Lightning Source LLC
Chambersburg PA
CBHW071506220526
45472CB00003B/929